LONDON'S GOLDEN JUBILEE BUSES

David Stewart

Capital Transport

ISBN 185414 264 X

Published in 2002 by
Capital Transport Publishing
38 Long Elmes
Harrow Weald
Middlesex

Printed by CS Graphics
Singapore

Capital Transport thanks
Ian Bell
Mike Weston
Nicky Cheshire
Nick Agnew
Michael Walton
and all the photographers
for their help.

The front cover photograph
is by Mark Lyons and the
title page photo by
Capital Transport

Left: Arriva Olympian 5127
at Harrow Weald.
Capital Transport

Contents

Right: It was not only the gold Routemasters that carried a conductor. Trident operated route 55 also has two-person crews. In April, fresh in its special livery, TA409 is seen in Oxford Street. *Ian Bell*

Introduction

As part of the celebrations to commemorate Her Majesty the Queen's Golden Jubilee, fifty London buses were turned out in gold livery during the spring of 2002.

In summer 2001 Transport for London were approached by the Golden Jubilee Office, set up to encourage projects for Jubilee year. TfL were asked if it would be possible to have some gold buses in 2002 in the same way that silver Routemasters had been turned out for the Queen's Silver Jubilee in 1977.

Fifty was the obvious number of vehicles to aim for and it was decided to seek sponsorship for the buses by selling exclusive advertising space inside and outside. The seeking of sponsors was handled by Viacom, the privatised company that handles the work once done by British Transport Advertising and London Transport Advertising. The advertising market was less buoyant at the start of 2002 than it had been in 1977 and, in addition there was a lot of scepticism about just how successful the Golden Jubilee celebrations were going to be – some feeling (very wrongly as things turned out) that the monarchy was less popular in 2002 than it had been in 1977 and that the event would be overshadowed by the football World Cup. It was decided to seek just five sponsors, each of which would pay £200,000 for a seven month contract on ten buses. The official start date for the contracts was 15th April. The potential sponsors were seen as falling into two main categories: those with a strong British heritage connection and companies or products celebrating their fiftieth anniversary in 2002. British Airways, British Gas and British Telecom declined, as did the troubled and cash-strapped Royal Mail.

The form the advertising would take was discussed with TfL. Viacom suggested what they called a branded swathe towards the back of each bus side coupled with an all-over rear advert. They also presented the standard T shape advertising as an option, but strongly recommended something more adventurous for the special occasion. Different shades of gold were considered and the choice was made of 'antique gold'. Advertisers were given the option of branded vinyl flooring and special moquette for the seat covering. Marks & Spencer considered this but in the event none of the advertisers took up either option. Apart from the standard interior advertising sites being devoted to the sponsor, no other work was done inside the buses.

London Taxis International, in association with TfL, also decided to arrange for fifty taxis to be painted gold. In this case they were all new vehicles delivered in gold and no sponsors were involved. To provide an incentive for taxi drivers to buy them, optional extras were included free of charge. The taxis were to stay in gold beyond 2002, minus Jubilee branding, and gold was to become an optional colour for taxis in future. Each of the fifty taxis carried a 'fleet number' indicating each year of the Queen's reign.

The official announcement about the impending fleet of fifty gold buses and fifty gold taxis was made on 18 January 2002 by the Mayor of London, Ken Livingstone. The London Tourist Board added a comment that "The Golden Jubilee is a fantastic opportunity to tempt back the overseas visitors that London lost in 2001" and hoped that the sight of golden buses and taxis would help to promote London as "the place to be in 2002".

There were concerns about the potential problems of using gold paint on buses, particularly the way in which gold paint shows up minor dents rather more than red does, and the problems of retouching following the inevitable scrapes in service – sheets of vinyl are more easily replaced. A major factor was that of the time needed to repaint a bus gold and then back to red again at the end of the contracts – the Golden Jubilee Office had specified that no gold buses should run in service beyond the end of 2002. There was also the need to avoid fifty buses being off the road for the time it would take to give a full repaint both at the start and end of the contracts.

The Golden Jubilee Office were keen that the London celebrations should be London-wide, whereas the sponsors would naturally be keen to see their buses in central London. A balance was struck that ensured suburban exposure as well as heavy presence in the main tourist and shopping thoroughfares. Four sponsors took up the opportunity, with TfL deciding to be the fifth. Marks & Spencer were the first commercial sponsor, followed by Unilever (Surf washing powder), Mars (Celebration Chocolates), and Nestle's (Felix cat food).

The buses were to be split between Routemasters and low-floor double deckers. Subsequently some intermediate designs of double decker were substituted for some of the low-floor vehicles in order to give some impression of the developments in design during the Queen's reign. This was particularly relevant when it was decided that five buses would take part in the pageant down The Mall on June 4th. The largest single type in the gold bus fleet was the Routemaster of which there were 15 – twelve RMLs and three RMs. In terms of numerical strength, these were equalled by 15 Dennis Tridents, although their bodywork was split between Alexander and Plaxton. Following were 10 Olympians, six Volvo B7TLs, two DAFs and single examples of a Volvo Citybus and a 23-year old Titan.

Interior sites

Left: The option of special moquette on the seats and printed vinyl floor covering was offered. Only Marks & Spencer gave serious consideration to this and in the event no-one took up either option.

Below: Spec Art showing a traditional T Side layout and the 'branded swathe' that was adopted.

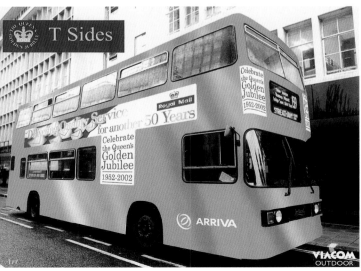

T Sides

Special sites

The work of applying the vinyls was carried out at Ash Grove garage, where these photographs were taken. The vinyl sheets were supplied with protective covering that was peeled off after they had been stuck on to the buses. Areas of the buses not suitable for vinyls were painted gold.
Ian Bell

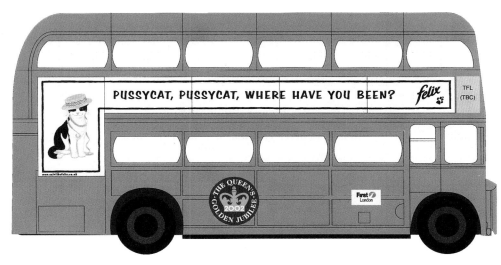

Visuals were prepared as guides to garage staff. In practice the positioning of the Golden Jubilee logos varied to some extent. The TfL branding, originally intended to appear below the front upper deck windows, was moved to the lower deck.

In practice, and to get as many buses completed as soon as possible, vinyl was applied in the weeks before the actual sponsorship advertising or the Golden Jubilee logos and TfL legends had been delivered. Therefore, during March and April several buses ran in service in plain gold. The very first to be seen in service was Arriva's RM6 on route 137 on Tuesday 12th March. Some weeks later, and after a vandalism attack at Brixton garage over the Easter weekend, this vehicle was to lose its vinyl in favour of real gold paint. Fourteen of the fifteen Routemasters (the exception was RML2305) plus Titan T172 were outshopped during March in plain gold, and very plain they looked at that stage. Shepherd's Bush garage applied 'normal' adverts into the frames on RML2414, no doubt by mistake, until the correct Felix adverts arrived. The more modern types followed, and they all first operated in service with the correct sponsorship adverts, although the earlier examples to be completed still had to wait a few weeks for the Jubilee logos and TfL legends to be applied. The positioning of these varied from bus to bus and on offsides from nearsides. Also, company fleetnames and fleet numbers were slow to appear in many cases, and indeed one or two buses never did receive their numbers.

Left: One of the fifty taxis painted gold. Each was dedicated to a particular year of the Queen's reign, displayed on the front doors. *Ian Bell*

Below: Four of the gold buses lined up at Trafalgar Square for a press showing on 29th April. *Ian Bell*

All fifty buses had been gilded by the second week of May, Connex's TA38 being the last. On 24th April RML2305 and TAL951 were at TfL's Victoria headquarters to be viewed by Transport Commissioner Bob Kiley, who had indicated concern about the appearance of some of the gold Routemasters he had seen running in service. Then the official launch occurred at Trafalgar Square on 29th April, attended by DLP50, TAL951, VPL219, TA50 and TA111. Each represented one of the five sponsors.

The mixture of gold vinyls and paint is in evidence in this detail view of RML2620 in Oxford Street. *Capital Transport*

One gold bus to be seen within Greater London that was not part of the TfL fleet was RM2107, owned by International Coaches Ltd of Thornton Heath. It was painted all over in common with RM6 and RT4712 which followed, and is seen in 'party bus' role at Epsom in May. *David Heath*

Left: Some of the gold buses ran in service for a short time before receiving the dedicated advertising. RM6 was at first given vinyls but these were removed after a few weeks and the bus was given a gold paint treatment instead. *Capital Transport*

Above: RML 2414 ran for a time in March with ordinary commercial advertising. Inside the gold buses when fully attired, the advertising was also for the sponsor. *Ian Bell*

The painting of RT4712 gold nears completion at Arriva's Enfield garage. Arriva looked after the bus during its period of Golden Jubilee service. It had originally been planned to have a red relief band and red wheels but when the red wheels were inspected, the plan changed to white relief with black wheels. *E. Milburn*

During the spring of 2002, arrangements were made to take RT4712, a long-term resident of the LT Museum, out for a period of service during Golden Jubilee Year. Arriva were given the job of renovating the vehicle and making it mechanically fit for service. The original idea of running it for a while on route 73 from Tottenham Garage was expanded to include other routes. The bus was completed during May, in fully painted gold rather than vinyl, and moved from Enfield Garage to the LT Museum at Acton on 21st May. In the following week it gained special blinds for the Jubilee Weekend and adverts 'Celebrating 50 Years of Road Safety' as befitting its sponsorship by TfL Street Management. It had red TfL fleetnames and numbers, and had specially made stencils for 'ER 50'. It was first shown in public at the Covent Garden Museum on 31st May, it featured in the Golden Jubilee Pageant along The Mall on 4th June, and at a Royal Visit to Willesden Bus Garage on 6th.

The RT appeared at the Museum's Open Days at Acton on 15/16th June, and on special tours on the next three Sundays. These tours left Covent Garden at 0930 and cost £50 a head – which included a guide/courier, lunch and any admission fees. 'River and Royalty' on 23rd June visited Greenwich, including a trip on the Woolwich Ferry, Westminster, past Royal Residences, to Hampton Court. A stop was made for lunch at the business park built on the site of Chiswick Works. Traffic delays meant that it could not make the last section on to Windsor Castle. 'Metroland' on 30th June went via Marylebone to Aylesbury and Quainton Road, but never reached the intended extent of the tour at Brill. '1940s/50s' on 7th July visited Croydon Airport,

Biggin Hill and Chartwell, although the bus only actually reached Westerham, a couple of miles short of its destination, for fear of tree damage. Special gold tickets were issued and special 'Tour' blinds were displayed.

Otherwise, the summer was punctuated with several special events which the RT attended. These included a visit to Holloway Garage open day on 22nd June, a hire by LOTS on Monday 22nd July where the original London sightseeing tour routes as had been operated in 1952 were re-created, the one-day-only route 441C (Hatton Cross–Staines–Windsor) on the occasion of the Bus of Yesteryear rally at Staines on 11th August and a visit to the East Anglia Transport Museum on 7th and 8th September.

Facing page: RT4712 partakes of a trip on the Woolwich Ferry on 23rd June. *Ian Bell*

Above: The RT at the site of Chiswick Works, recently redeveloped as a business park. *Ian Bell*

Left: RT4712 is overtaken by a Metrobus Dart at Westerham. *Ian Bell*

Above: During the Metroland tour a visit was made to the Buckinghamshire Railway Centre at Quainton Road. *Ian Bell*

Left: A special ticket was printed for the day tours organised by London's Transport Museum.

The RT took part in the Bus of Yesteryear Rally on 11th August on a special service linking Windsor and Hatton Cross via the site of the rally, Staines bus station. It was intended to do four round trips but the bus could not complete the schedule owing to overheating. RML2414 was one of the other buses on the service and RML2431 worked tours around Heathrow Airport. *Mark Lyons*

The Golden Jubilee Pageant

Events over the Golden Jubilee Holiday long weekend included the Golden Jubilee Pageant on 4th June. The 'Services Parade' section included six gold vehicles, one from each of the six largest operators, and featuring each of the sponsors. Led by First's red open-top RMC 1510, the convoy consisted (in running order) of RT4712 (manned by Arriva), RML2405 (First/ Felix), RML2450 (Stagecoach/M&S), T172 (Go Ahead/TfL), VPL219 (Metroline/Surf) and TA224 (London United/Chocolates). Arriva's newly painted RM6 was in the 'History Parade' section of the pageant.

Facing page: The vehicles taking part in the pageant spent the morning parked on Westminster Bridge. In this view, the convoy of buses enter Parliament Square in the direction of Horse Guards Parade.
E. Milburn

This page: RT4712 and RML2450 play their part in the pageant watched by thousands of flag-waving spectators.

The gold bus cavalcade in the Jubilee Pageant on 4th June passes the royal family in front of Buckingham Palace. Though cloudy, the weather stayed dry until the end of the pageant. The first of these two photographs was taken from the upper deck of open top Routemaster RMC1510.
Mike Weston/Nick Agnew

The 'running number' ER 50 was carried by the RT on special occasions. *Ian Bell*

Inside the RT, posters in similar style to ones carried in buses at the time of the Coronation were displayed. *Ian Bell*

The Gold Buses in Service

When the sponsorship of the fifty gold buses was arranged, perhaps it was envisaged that 'the message' would be broadcast along specific routes. While this was maintained in many cases, some garages tended to allocate the buses as they would any other, i.e. to any suitable route.

Given that there are only a few crew routes, the fifteen Routemasters were of course route-bound. Well, almost! Those allocated to the 8, 10, 11, 12, 36, 38 and 73 stayed there as they were the only crew routes at their garages, but those allocated to garages who had two crew routes were used indiscriminately. Therefore, at Brixton (routes 137/159), Putney (14/22), Shepherd's Bush (9/94), Westbourne Park (7/23) and Willesden

(6/98), the buses could be on either route – and often two of them on the same route. First's RM1650 (alias SRM3) was used on a couple of special services: on Easter Sunday 31st March it ran journeys on the 25, 179 and 369 in east London, while on 25th May, in conjunction with a school fete at Perivale, it displayed E5 blinds and took fete visitors on trips to nearby Greenford. One other crew bus to mention was Leyton's TA409 – being dedicated to route 55 by virtue of its lack of ticket equipment and restricted blind display, it was always to be found on that service.

Reviewing the other vehicles and starting with Arriva, VA157 was invariably on route 24 except that it made one Sunday trip

When the first gold buses started to appear on the streets in March, they looked incredibly plain and seemed very dull. The sole 'Marshall' refurbished RM to receive gold was RM1650, numerically if not actually (due to body changes during overhauls) one of those in Silver Jubilee livery in 1977. To recall this event, it carried small red fleet numbers SRM3, its identity in 1977. Without any other identity visible, it worked special journeys on routes 25, 179 and 369 on Easter Sunday 31st March, and is pictured arriving at Thames View Estate, Barking. Eight weeks later and now properly dressed, on 25th May it was used to give free rides over the E5 route on the occasion of a school fete at Medway Estate, Perivale. *Kevin Smith/David Heath*

on the 243 in July and an appearance on the 73 one Sunday in September, but Enfield's DLP2 could be on the 149 or 279. Wood Green's DLP50 was almost always on the 29, but made occasional excursions to the 141, 144, 221 and W3. London South's elderly Olympian L170 was hardly ever away from route 2. Indeed, its appearances on routes 68 or 176 – its intended home – could be counted on the fingers of one hand. The other Olympian 5127 was meant to be on the 142, but was just as often to be seen on the 340. Connex Bus had two Tridents, both for route 3. While TA5 was usually on the 3, TA38 was almost always to be found on the 196, occasionally on the 60 or 157, and sometimes on the 3 alongside TA5. East Thames Buses had one Olympian for route 180, but it made short visits north of the river for Ilford area services, mostly being used on the 150.

First's VN94 was almost always on route 83, and TAL951 on the 25; even so, VN94 did wander at least once to the 92 and twice to the 258, while TAL951 seemed to be a popular choice for the odd weekend rail replacement job – it managed to get as far out as Stansted Airport on one occasion. Northumberland Park's TN1113 and VN246 were allocated to the 91 and 341 respectively, and they were usually found thereon. Wanderings from those routes were quite unusual (although VN246 was known to have worked on the 76, 215, 259 and W8 at least once each), though it was not unknown for both to be on the same route (either 91 or 341, that is) on the same day. Similarly, TN832 and TN963 were allocated to the 18 and 27 respectively and, while they did usually stay put, there were occasions when they swapped routes or were both on the same route together. Here, we have an example of a Sunday variation where either one could sometimes be seen on Sundays on the 23.

Go-Ahead's London Central and General companies had a fair spread of gold buses, and route allocations were the most varied. AVL13 was meant to be on the 45, but was just as likely to be seen on the 35 or 40, as well as the 12 on Sundays. NV58 was meant for the 21 at New Cross, but it was mostly on the 172 instead, sometimes on the 171, or on the 36, both in weekday crew mode or opo on Sundays. Stockwell's two buses, NV128 and PVL257 were usually on the 133 and 345 respectively, but could also be seen on routes such as the 37, 77A or the weekend 11. The PVL was officially for the 77A but that was by far the rarest route. Putney's NV175 was 'dedicated' to route 74, but made odd visits to the 14 or the 170. The star item in the fleet was Titan T172 but it did tend to confine itself to peak hour work on the 63 or 381, in between

special jobs for the Commercial Services operation. Metrobus had just one gold bus, and it was always on the dedicated 64 – until August, that is, when it shared its time with route 119. Apparently representations were made from certain quarters in Bromley that their town had no gold buses running there – which was true – and this change was to address this.

London United is legendary in enthusiast circles for its propensity for oddities. Fulwell's two gold Tridents were meant to run on the 131 and 267, but could just as easily be seen radiating from Kingston on the 65, 71, 85, 281 or 411. Hounslow's VP130 was just as widespread, with the 337 to Clapham Junction often being substituted for routes such as the 111 to Heathrow or 120 to Northolt. Metroline were more cautious, with TPL268, VPL163, VPL188 and VPL219 being allocated to routes 82, 43, 52 and 113 respectively. That's not to say that they didn't wander, because they did; but not very often. TPL268 was seen in St Albans two or three times on route 84, VPL163 took to the W7 or 134 on occasions, VPL188 was sometimes on the 6 or 98 in evenings or Sundays; VPL219 made one appearance on the 204. At Stagecoach, Leyton's appropriately numbered TA1 and TA50 were allocated to the 48 and 56 but were frequently on the 58 or 69 instead. Upton Park's TA96 for the 115 could also be on the 101, 104, 238 or 330, and was often on the 15 on Sundays. TA111 was spread between the 26 and 30, and ran at least once on the 86. Selkent's TA140 and VN95 were allocated for the 53 and 54 respectively, but wandering was not so common. Nonetheless, the TA did get onto the 99 at times and the VN onto the 47, 136 or 160.

Did they go outside Greater London in service? Yes, but – other than the 142 to Watford or working back to Potters Bar after running on the 82 – not really intentionally. Places such as West Molesey in Surrey (route 411), St Albans in Hertfordshire (84) and Chigwell Row in Essex (150) saw isolated gold buses in service, and probably Dartford in Kent (route 96).

The relatively small night allocation compared with the day allocation inevitably meant that the likelihood of a gold bus on a night route was reduced. The biggest night allocations of the same type of bus were on the N25 and N29, and those were the likeliest places to find a gold bus, although there was the possibility within the smaller allocations on routes such as the N3, N14, N18, N27 and N91. One garage that did often put a gold bus out at night was Stockwell, with occasional visits to routes such as N37, N44, N77, N88 or N345.

'There's a great deal to celebrate' it says on the side of RM6. Apart from the Golden Jubilee itself, the advert was really an exhortation from TfL to remind everyone that 'Buses are getting better'. When painted, RM6 had a white relief band added, the only RM so treated. *Philip Wallis*

On RM25 Surf's '50 spotless years' seemed to have greater prominence than the Queen's 50 years in its advertisement. The positioning of the TfL and operator logos was often in different places on different buses. Brixton's two RMs shared their time on routes 137 and 159, and here the 159 via point display is incorrectly shown. *Capital Transport*

It is July 2002, and the familiar location at the south side of Trafalgar Square has yet to be altered. By the autumn this famous photographic spot was changed and the road layout made two-way. RM1650 is among those to have been fitted with hopper windows in place of the original ones and by July it had, like its red brethren, gained bright yellow spots on the mirrors (to make them more visible!). *Stephen Madden*

Several of London Central's RMLs had hopper window conversions, including golden RML2283, at Marble Arch on route 36 heading back home to points south of the River. The contrast in colour can be seen between the painted side window frames and the vinyl. *Stephen Madden*

Hyde Park Corner on Sunday 2nd June, and RML2305 works route 14, one of several routes that reverted to crew operation in recent years. It has yet to gain a fleet number, and has had its cab door painted rather than vinyled, perhaps as a result of damage? *Colin Brown*

Three gold RMLs have '50' as part of their fleet number – which was not a coincidence. Tottenham's RML2350 crosses Oxford Circus with a totally different fleetname style to that on the same company's RMs 6 and 25 seen earlier. *Kevin Smith*

Westbourne Park was one of five garages that had either more than one gold bus or more than one crew route. Therefore RML2405, the sole RML to carry a red fleet number, could be seen equally on routes 7 or 23. On 15th July it is in Oxford Street on route 7. *Geoff Rixon*

London United adopted their house style, with yellow fleet numbers and the fleetname above the cab instead of on the lower body sides. Felix-sponsored RML2414 stalks another RML on the 9 at Hyde Park Corner on 15th June.
Stephen Madden

Before going into gold, Metroline's RML2431 had been a 'special' in the fleet, as it was a trial vehicle for a new engine/gearbox combination which has led to a similar adoption on many other buses. The Routemasters had their grille and bonnet areas painted, due to the difficulty of applying awkward shapes of vinyl, and one can see the slightly different shades of gold. *Colin Brown*

Left: There were three RMLs sponsored by Marks & Spencer, and the slogan on the nearside differed slightly from that on the offside. RML2450 traverses Shoreditch High Street, a location which had disrupted route 8 for much of the year due to road works. *Philip Wallis*

Right: London Central's RML2499, pictured in Peckham, shows evidence of gold touch-up paint around the bus lane camera, and needs a bit more round the headlight! It is also the only gold RML that ran through the summer without a fleetname. *Colin Stannard*

Celebration Chocolates shower the side advertising on RML2600 as it turns at Oxford Circus. On the occasion of the Hounslow Garage open day on Saturday 14th September, the bus was loaned and used on route 81. *Gerald Mead*

When the Routemasters were first treated to gold vinyl in March and April, fleet numbers were omitted. One vehicle that stayed number-less was Holloway's RML2620, shown in this June Oxford Street view. *Colin Brown*

RML2648 opposite St Paul's Cathedral is still carrying its RA (Waterloo) garage code in this picture, prior to route 11's RMLs moving to Stockwell from 25th May. Note the amount of gold touch-up paint around most of the windows! *Kevin Smith*

Right: Another with a painted cab door is RML2750, like sister bus RML2350 with a large Arriva name and the orange Arriva 'swirl' logo. It spent its time on route 38, and enters Piccadilly at Hyde Park Corner on 26th June. *Stephen Madden*

The sole gold Titan was T172, but was slightly different in that it had two thin black bands top and bottom of the between-decks area. The nearside of the vehicle, with its painted doors, is seen as it forces its way across lines of traffic at King's Cross. In the offside view, compare the application of the TfL sponsorship with that on the RMLs. The bus was often taken off service to work at special events, like the Wimbledon Tennis services in June. T172 was usually confined in service to peak hour duties on either route 63 or 381, but on one Sunday in September it did make a rare visit to route 36.
Colin Stannard/David Heath

Another one-off was the sole Alexander bodied Volvo Citybus to appear in gold. VA157, which received incorrect fleet number V157 on both sides, was invariably to be found on route 24. The position of an inspection panel (nearside) and emergency door (offside) has caused the Surf 50-years label to be stuck in different places.
Gerald Mead/Kevin Smith

An elderly Olympian was perhaps a surprising choice for the gold treatment, but L170 – complete with its former RM registration – was done. Intended for route 176, it was almost exclusively on route 2 instead. It was also the only gold bus to have 'normal' adverts pasted either side of the blind box, in the place that would have Golden Jubilee symbols, had there been room! Short working destinations are displayed in both pictures, going to Marble Arch at Queen Mother's Gate, Park Lane, and at Stockwell.
Steve Maskell/Gerald Mead

Arriva the Shires had one of only two TfL gold buses that were based outside Greater London, in this case at Garston Garage. Their Olympian No.5127 (formerly LR97) was used equally on routes 142 and 340 in north-west London, and is pictured at Brent Cross on 17th June. If you look very closely, the tiny turquoise 'serving the Shires & Essex' legend under the Arriva name had by this time replaced the more appropriate 'serving London' carried in its first few weeks in gold. *Gerald Mead*

Above: As with the RMLs, the M&S slogans differed on both sides of their sponsored vehicles. Photographed on 2nd May before the bus gained its fleetnames, numbers and TfL legends, First's VN 94 serves 'the heart of the community' in West Ealing.
Gerald Mead

Left: A miniature Stagecoach fleetname, and lack of any frontal adornment – except for the customary front upper-deck window etching sadly normal in this part of London – VN 95 travels through Lewisham. Route 54 was its normal haunt, although it did work on Catford's other routes at times.
Kevin Smith

First London's Volvo Olympian VN 246 was one of its batch that was still in the old Capital yellow livery before being treated to gold. Normally on route 341, it certainly did wander at times to other north London routes, as evidenced by this appearance on route 259 at Finsbury Park. *Capital Transport*

Sadly, the prominent Golden Jubilee discs on the fronts of Routemasters were not able to be applied on the Olympians. NV58 was announced as being allocated to route 21, but in practice it was on route 172 nearly the whole time, as shown here in Waterloo. *Colin Stannard*

Stockwell's NV128 was widely spread and, although intended for the 133, was used frequently on routes 37 and 77A as well as on the 11 at weekends and on occasional night workings. The bus travels down the Strand on route 77A. *Kevin Smith*

Right: London General's NV175 was the sole 'Palatine 2' bodied Olympian treated to gold, and it was normally on route 74, as shown by this view on Putney Bridge. *Ian Bell*

East Thames Buses had just one gold bus, East Lancs bodied Olympian No.372. Meant for route 180, it is seen thereon in Lewisham. The old nursery rhyme 'Pussy Cat, Pussy Cat, where have you been? I've been up to London to look at the Queen' is a little inappropriate for this out-of-town vehicle, which would never reach central London on the 180. It also worked in ETB's other area, and was captured in Gants Hill on route 150 on 15th May. In September, ETB took on some peak journeys on route 53 and so No.372 made it to Westminster. *Kevin Smith/Gerald Mead*

Unlike ETB's East Lancs Olympian, 'Metrobus' No.850 had a bold blue fleetname on the front. Once route-bound on the 64, it also worked the 119 from August, but was still the only gold bus to work regularly in the Croydon area, where these views were taken.
Laurie Rufus/Kevin Smith

Three operators had gold TAs – all ALX400 bodied Tridents, although their fleet numbering systems, lengths and door arrangements were not quite the same! Each applied Jubilee logos and names slightly differently, too. The lowest numbered Stagecoach Trident, TA1, is in Gracechurch Street in The City. *Colin Stannard*

With the staircase position in a different place on the earlier Connex Tridents, the Jubilee logo was also in a different position. TA5 in Whitehall was on its habitual route 3. *Gerald Mead*

The last of the fifty TfL buses to be given the gold treatment, and not until mid-May, was 'Connex' TA38, and it made its usual home on suburban route 196 between Brixton and Norwood Junction. This view graphically shows the problems of photographing ALX400s in midday summer sunshine – the shading over the blind box renders part of the blind barely readable. *Geoff Rixon*

Stagecoach's TAs all had a painted front lower panel, which somewhat brightens up this view in a dismal Bishopsgate in early June. Although seen on route 48, Leyton's pair (TA1 and 50) were actually allocated freely over routes 48, 56, 58 and 69. *Kevin Smith*

Opposite: TA96 was officially allocated to route 115, but in practice it was often instead on the 101, 104, 238 or 330, as well as the 15 on Sundays. One such wandering was on 29th July at Stratford. *Mark Lyons*

TA111 calls at Baker Street Station on route 30. The non-standard registration gives no obvious clue to the absent fleet number. *Steve Maskell*

TA140, also with Stagecoach, is seen in Belmont Hill, Lewisham in August. Route 53 was diverted through Lewisham for much of the year, due to a road collapse at Blackheath Hill. Oxford Circus, where it is bound, was something of a hub for gold buses, with 18 of the routes serving it normally having one or two.
Mark Lyons

London United had two gold Tridents on outer south-west London routes, and were meant to be on routes 131 and 267. The company took over route 65 on 29th June, and a few weeks later gold TA224 duly appeared at Ealing Broadway. *Colin Brown*

Continuing the usual London United practice of 'spreading it about', this Kingston view of TA225 shows the bus on route 85 on 28th June – the company's last day on the route. *Stephen Madden*

On 12th May, before many buses gained all their logos and lettering, TA409 prepares to return from Oxford Street to its home base at Leyton. Route 55 is conductor operated, as advertised by the posters alongside the blind box.
Kevin Smith

FirstGroup at Westbourne Park had two Tridents in gold, TN832 and TN963. TN832 was nominally for the 18 and TN963 for the 27. Appearances were also made on the 23, especially on Sundays, when the route is one-person operated. TN832 is shown at Euston and TN963 at Piccadilly Circus.
Colin Stannard

Unlike earlier TNs with First, later examples had narrower blind boxes. TN1113 spent nearly all of its time on route 91, here arriving at the Trafalgar Square terminus of the route. TN1113 had its moment of fame when it led the London contingent of gold buses in the 'Jubilee Gold Run' to Showbus at Duxford on 22nd September. Almost thirty gold buses from around the country took part, other London vehicles being TA225, RM6, RT4712, Metrobus 850, T172 and RML2283. *Mark Lyons*

Arriva had two Plaxton President bodied DAFs in gold, both with Felix sponsorship. Enfield's DLP2 was used on routes 149 or 279, and here it is far from home on the long 149, in The City near Monument Station. *Kevin Smith*

Arriva's other DLP, number 50, heads south into Charing Cross Road past Centre Point. Many of Arriva's modern buses have part of the fleet number repeated on the front, to aid identification now that registrations no longer match. The rear and nearside corner was badly damaged on 12th September when a motorcyclist crashed into it. The bus was due to return to service after a few weeks under repair. *Kevin Smith*

London Central's AVL13 in April lacked all its names and logos, although that was later rectified. Used on routes 12, 35, 40 and 45, it was pictured in Gresham Road, Brixton. *Geoff Rixon*

The blind fastening seems to have come adrift on TAL951 in this view in Ilford Town Centre. The bus was almost always on route 25, although it did escape at times! *Gerald Mead*

A Felix bus that only rarely (i.e. on Sundays or at night) 'went up to London to look at the Queen' was Hounslow Garage's VP130. It was more usually in the suburbs on the 111, 120 or 337, typified by this appearance on the edge of Greater London in Hampton on 8th May. *Geoff Rixon*

This rather unsatisfactory stand at Friern Barnet on route 43 was due to be removed to a new location in due course, but it was still in use through the 'gold bus reign' in 2002. VPL163 was one of three similar gold President bodied Volvo B7TLs with Metroline. *Dave Manning*

VPL188 from Willesden Garage spent almost its whole time there on route 52, shown here in Grosvenor Gardens, Victoria. Low light on the sides of the bus shows up the colour-shade variation on the repainted front lower panel. *Kevin Smith*

All three of Metroline's gold VPLs worked on major trunk routes, and the 113 was one of the longest, coming into central London all the way from Edgware. VPL 219 is seen at both ends of the route in May. *Kevin Smith/Capital Transport*

Route 82 from Potters Bar Garage had its VPLs (Volvos) replaced by TPLs (Tridents) in 2002, although the President bodywork was outwardly similar. At Journey's End at Victoria on 31st May, TPL 268 has just completed its lengthy trip.
Gerald Mead

PVL 257, in spite of being allotted to the 77A on the TfL 'gold allocation', it was actually one of a batch of London Central PVLs that were diverted to London General to convert route 345 to double-deck in spring 2002. It stayed on the route after most of its sisters moved on later in the summer, and shows off the new style of side blind (with intermediate points only) near Brixton. *Colin Brown*

The use of the gold buses on night routes was inevitably less well recorded, but it is known that Stockwell's vehicles made a number of appearances. PVL257 is seen at Trafalgar Square early one July morning. *Philip Wallis*

The Notting Hill Carnival on 25th and 26th August saw the use of RML2431 on route 52 and RML2499 on the special 12X service. One round trip by RM1650 on route 18 between the Prince of Wales and Euston was also made on the 25th. RML2431 is seen at Victoria. *Kevin Smith*

Gold RT Routes

There was a series of appearances of RT4712 on various central London crew routes during June, July and August. It had been planned to appear only during the Tuesdays, Wednesdays and Thursdays of each week, but not necessarily on all days. One problem that restricted its actual length of time on the road was the need to collect the bus each Tuesday morning from the Museum at Acton, followed by type-training of the drivers (different drivers each week, of course), and then the need to return it to Acton on each Thursday afternoon. The Museum, very much in a 'mother hen' role, were fussy about where and when it ran, so it didn't work on any of the routes in the evenings and they were worried about it running south of the River – fears of vandalism and window etching, most prevalent in that part of London, saw to that. London General declined an invitation to have the bus for route 11.

In the event, each garage did something different and did not necessarily work on all days, nor the full route in many cases. Mostly, it was on a 'supplementary' running to the normal schedule, but in others (e.g. when on route 7) it substituted for a scheduled RML working. The essential point was that it should be a fairly low-key operation, not detracting from the impact of the main fleet of fifty sponsored gold buses. It was hoped to 'delight' and 'surprise' passers-by and passengers by its random and sudden appearances, although the rather unscientific practice of just riding on the bus seemed to reveal that most passengers were blissfully unaware of its significance. Not so the crews who were special volunteers, all of whom had worked on the RT family many years previously.

A composite blind set was made, mostly with 1950s style upper-case lettering on the 'via point' displays. Some had four-line and some five-line displays and, as befitting route 23's status as a 'new route' its display was in lower-case style. The ultimate blinds included only the final destinations, but here there was a problem in that many of the journeys actually operated were short workings, and in any case points such as 'Hammersmith' (route 9) and Willesden (route 6) were unfortunately omitted. It did have final destinations for the 38 and 73, but all the 73s and all but one 38 journey worked to short points such as Islington and Tottenham Court Road. The display 'Special Service' was thus in use on quite a number of journeys. Route 15 was a late addition to the list, by special request of Upton Park staff.

18/19/20 June.
73 (Tottenham) – It ran on the Tuesday afternoon, for most of the day on Wednesday and a round-trip on Thursday morning.

25/26/27 June.
38 (Clapton) – It ran between about 0900-1830 on Tuesday and Wednesday, but not at all on the Thursday. On both the 73 and 38, most journeys were short workings from the Victoria end, mostly as far as Islington or Tottenham Court Road only.

2/3/4 July.
23 (Westbourne Park) – It did three full route round trips, on the Tuesday afternoon peak, on Wednesday afternoon and again on Thursday morning.

9/10/11 July.
8 (Bow) – There was one eastbound journey from Victoria to Bow on Tuesday, whilst being delivered to Bow from Acton. Then, problems with the brakes meant that it only did one of the planned three round-trips on the next two days, one in the Wednesday afternoon peak.

16/17/18 July.
9 (Shepherd's Bush) – Here, it ran only on Wednesday, with one round trip from Hammersmith to Aldwych, one short journey to Hyde Park Corner and one to Green Park. An Underground strike on Thursday and fears of overloading prevented its use.

23/24/25 July.
159 (Brixton) – The intended operation was deferred to 11/12 September when one round trip was made on each day.

30/31 July and 1 August.
7 (Westbourne Park) – It ran one afternoon round trip on the Wednesday and again on the Thursday.

6/7/8 August.
6 (Willesden) – This was by far the most extensive and 'normal' operation, with seven full route round-trips and with little problems with road works, etc, ensuring that the intended journeys were all achieved. Two trips on Tuesday, three on Wednesday and two on Thursday.

13/14/15 August.
15 (Upton Park) – It ran on Wednesday only, with two round-trips between Aldgate and Paddington, and one from Aldgate to Charing Cross. It ran light between the garage and Aldgate.

Vintage style blinds had been made for eight of the nine routes that RT4712 was due to work during the summer. Most blind displays had upper case lettering, featuring plenty of abbreviations – something which used to be much more common than is the case today. Unfortunately, many of the journeys actually worked were short workings, correct destinations were not always available, and so the 'Special Service' display was sometimes used. Route 73 was the vehicle's first genuine route in the summer of 2002. *Mark Lyons*

On route 38 in the second week, the bus heads for Victoria with a five-line blind, on one side of Hyde Park Corner, and back to 'Special Service' (actually Islington) on the other side, entering Piccadilly. *Stephen Madden*

The rather less traditional route 23 saw a more modern style of blind, and it is seen with its interior light bulbs illuminated, in spite of the lucky flashes of sunshine in these views. First passing through the City of London on Threadneedle Street, once the scene of trials of its wider (RTW) brethren over fifty years ago, it is seen a little later going away from the photographer at Trafalgar Square.
Kevin Smith/ Stephen Madden

Next it was the turn of route 8 and Bow Garage, who made use of an old Gibson ticket machine to add to the period flavour. The blinds for some of these special workings included via points not previously seen on RTs, such as Berkeley Square. This photograph was taken at Green Park. *Nick Agnew*

London United had the RT in the fifth week for route 9. It was used on Wednesday 17th July, but did not run on the next day due to a Tube strike, leading to fears of overloading and heavy congestion putting too much of a strain on the elderly bus. Our view shows the bus at Hyde Park Corner. *Kevin Smith*

On route 7 with First London, the RT was captured here in Oxford Street on 31st July, when it did one complete round trip including working from and back to Westbourne Park garage in service. Coincidentally another of First's gold buses is following behind. *Capital Transport*

When Metroline used the RT on route 6, weather conditions varied from hot sunshine to heavy rain. Seen here at the western end of Oxford Street and again at Kensal Rise, where it is crewed by Eugene Collymore and Olive Murray, both of whom helped show the Queen around Willesden Garage on her Jubilee Visit there on 6th June.
Stephen Madden/ Nick Agnew

Route 15 was added to the list at the request of staff at Upton Park Garage. It had not been included on the specially made blinds but a set of RT blinds was borrowed from a private owner, enabling it to be properly turned out. The RT is seen packed with peak hour passengers at Marble Arch on Wednesday afternoon 14th August. *Geoff Rixon*

Originally planned for July, the operation of RT4712 on the 159 was deferred until 11th and 12th September. On the 11th, the bus is seen in Oxford Street nearing the end of its single round trip to Brixton Garage. *Capital Transport*

At the Rear

'Super Rear' advertising is established on London buses, but the front-entrance Golden Jubilee buses had a continuation of this around the sides to the rear wheels. The photographs on this and the following four pages show the five advertising messages at the rear. On Routemasters the standard advertising site was used. L170 ran for a short time with an incorrect spelling of the word Jubilee, as shown in the first picture.
Colin Lloyd/Stephen Madden/ Capital Transport